International Workshop on EUV Lithography 2017

Berkeley, California, USA
12 - 15 June 2017

ISBN: 978-1-5108-5018-7

Printed from e-media with permission by:

Curran Associates, Inc.
57 Morehouse Lane
Red Hook, NY 12571

CURRAN ASSOCIATES INC. proceedings.com

Some format issues inherent in the e-media version may also appear in this print version.

Printed by Curran Associates, Inc. (2018)

For permission requests, please contact EUV Litho, Inc.
at the address below.

EUV Litho, Inc.
10202 Wommack Road
Austin, TX 78748
USA

Phone: (512) 462-2290
Fax: (512) 462-1898

http://euvlitho.com

Additional copies of this publication are available from:

Curran Associates, Inc.
57 Morehouse Lane
Red Hook, NY 12571 USA
Phone: 845-758-0400
Fax: 845-758-2633
Email: curran@proceedings.com
Web: www.proceedings.com

2017 International Workshop on EUV Lithography

(2017 EUVL Workshop)

CXRO, LBNL, Berkeley, CA, USA
June 12-15, 2017

Workshop Proceedings

Wednesday, June 14, 2017

8:00 AM Welcome and Introduction

Session 1: Keynote – 1

Session Chair: Anthony Yen (ASML)

Break (20 minutes)

Session 2: EUV Masks and Mask Metrology

Session Co-chairs: Jim Wiley (ASML) and Bryan Kasprowicz (Photronics)

Lunch 12:20 AM – 1:20 PM

Session 3: EUV Sources- I

Session Co-chairs: Akira Endo (HiLASE) and Oscar Versolato (ARCNL)

Break and Group Photograph 2:20 PM (30 Minutes)

Session 4: EUV Sources - II

Session Chair: *Erik R. Hosler (GLOBALFOUNDRIES) and Hiroshi Kawata (KEK)*

Session 5: Poster Session 5:30 7:00 PM

Session Chair: *Gregory Denbeaux (SUNPU Poly)*

Takeo Watanabe and Tetsuo Harada
Center for EUVL, Laboratory of Advanced Science and Technology for Industry, University of Hyogo

Aamod Shanker
Dept. of Electrical Engineering and Computer Sciences, University of California, Berkeley, CA

Yow-Gwo Wang,[a,b,*] Andrew R. Neureuther,[a,b] Patrick P. Naulleau[b]
[a]*University of California, Berkeley, Department of Electrical Engineering and Computer Sciences, Berkeley, California, United States, 94720*
[b]*Lawrence Berkeley National Laboratory, Center for X-ray Optics, 1 Cyclotron Road, Berkeley, California, United States, 94720*

Xiangzhao Wang*, Heng Zhang, Sikun Li
Laboratory of Information Optics and Opto-electronic Technology, Shanghai Institute of Optics and Fine Mechanics, Chinese Academy of Sciences, Shanghai, China, 201800

Winner of First Place in the Poster Session
Young Woong Kim[1], Dong Gon Woo[1], Seung Hyuk Shin[2], Hoon Jo[2], Whoi-Yul Kim[2] and Jinho Ahn[1]
[1]*Division of Materials Science and Engineering*
[2]*Department of Electronics and Computer Engineering*
Hanyang University, 222 Wangsimni-ro, Seongdong-gu, Seoul 04763, Republic of Korea

Jan Bußmann[1,2], Michal Odstrcil[1,3], Raoul Bresenitz[1], Yusuke Teramoto[4], Marco Perske[5], Torsten Feigl[5], William S. Brocklesby[3], Larissa Juschkin[1,2]
[1] *Chair for Experimental Physics of EUV, JARA-FIT, RWTH Aachen University, Steinbachstrasse 15, 52074 Aachen, Germany*
[2] *Peter Grünberg Institute 9, JARA-FIT, Forschungszentrum Jülich GmbH, 52425 Jülich, Germany*
[3] *Optoelectronics Research Center, University of Southampton, SO17 1BJ, United Kingdom*
[4] *BLV Licht- und Vakuumtechnik GmbH, Steinbachstraße 15, Aachen, Germany*
[5] *OptiXfab. GmbH, Hans-Knoell-Str. 6, 07745 Jena, Germany*

End Day 1

Thursday, June 15, 2017

Welcome and Announcements (Intro-2)
Patrick Naulleau, LBL

Session 6: Keynote-2

Session Chair: Patrick Naulleau (LBL)

Break (20 Minutes)

Session 7: Optics and Contamination

Session Co-Chairs: Jan van Schoot (ASML) and Ladislav Pina (RITE

EUV/SXR Optics and Metrology Development at RITE (P24) (Invited Paper) 23
Ladislav Pina
Rigaku Innovative Technologies Europe (RITE), Prague, Czech Republic

Lunch 12:00 PM (60 Minutes)

Steering Committee working lunch meeting (Closed meeting)

Session 8: Resist and Patterning -1

Session Co-Chairs: Greg McIntyre (IMEC) and Yoshi Hishiro (JSR)

EUVL Developments at Imec (P47) (Invited Paper) 40
Greg McIntyre
IMEC

Reactivity of Metal Oxalate EUV Resists as a Function of the Central Metal (P41) (Invited Paper) 35
Steven Grzeskowiak,[a] Amrit Narasimhan,[a] Michael Murphy,[a] Lee Napolitano,[b] Daniel A. Freedman,[b] Robert L. Brainard,[a] and Greg Denbeaux[a]
[a] *State University of New York Polytechnic Institute - CNSE, 257 Fuller Rd. Albany, NY 12203*
[b] *State University of New York at New Paltz, 1 Hawk Drive New Paltz, NY 12561*

Novel EUV resist development for sub-7 nm node (P43) (Invited Paper) 37
Yoshi Hishiro
JSR Micro INC, 1280 N. Mathilda Ave, Sunnyvale, CA 94089, USA

Metal Oxide Photoresists: Breaking Paradigms in EUV Lithography (P50) (Invited Paper) 42
Jason Stowers
Inpria

Fundamental Aspect of Photosensitized Chemically Amplified Resist: How to overcome RLS trade-off (P46) (Invited Paper) .....N/A
Seiichi Tagawa[1,2]
[1]*Graduate School of Engineering, Osaka University, Ibaraki, Osaka 567-0047, Japan,*
[2]*Institute of Scientific and Industrial Research, Osaka University, Ibaraki, Osaka 567-0047, Japan*

Break 2:50 PM (20 Minutes)

Session 9: Resist and Patterning -2

Session Co-chairs: Greg Denbeaux (SUNY Poly) and Frank Ogletree (LBL)

Alex Hexemer
Lawrence Berkeley National Laboratory, Berkeley, California, United States, 94720

S. Castellanos[a], Y. Zhang[a], J. Haitjema[a], L. Wu[a], O. Luigier[a], D. Kazazis[b], M. Vockenhuber[b], T. R. Fallica[b], Y. Ekinci[b], A.M. Brouwer[a].
[a] *Advaced Research Center for Nanolithography, Science Park 110, 1098XG Amsterdam, The Netherlands*
[b] *Paul Scherrer Institute, 5232 Villigen PSI, Switzerland*

D. Frank Ogletree
Molecular Foundry, Materials Sciences Division, Lawrence Berkeley National Laboratory, 1 Cyclotron Road, Berkeley CA 94720 USA

Dan Slaughter
Chemical Sciences Division, LBNL

Vivek Bakshi
EUV Litho, Inc.

Depart for Dinner

6:00 -9:00 PM Dinner Cruise

EUV
LITHO, INC.

2017 International Workshop on EUV Lithography

June 12-15, 2017

CXRO, LBNL ▪ Berkeley, CA

Workshop Abstracts

EUV
LITHO, INC.

Sponsors

Organized by

Vivek Bakshi (EUV Litho, Inc.), Chair
Patrick Naulleau (CXRO), Co-Chair

Contents

Welcome

Dear Colleagues;

I would like to welcome you to the 10th year of International Workshop on EUV Lithography (EUVL Workshop) at CXRO in Berkeley, CA! EUVL workshop continues its focus on R&D topics and we are looking forward to an excellent agenda, discussions and networking.

This workshop has been made possible by the support of workshop sponsors, steering committee members, workshop support staff, session chairs and presenters. I would like to thank them for their contributions and for making this workshop a success. I look forward to your participation.

Best Regards

Vivek Bakshi
Chair, 2017 International Workshop on EUVL (2017 EUVL Workshop)

Abstracts

(Listed by Paper number)

P1

EUVL: Current Status & Remaining Challenges

(Keynote Presentation)

Obert R Wood II

GLOBALFOUNDRIES
400 Stone Break Road Extension, Malta, New York 12020, U.S.A.

Advantages of EUV lithography are wide process windows, high throughput and extendibility. Disadvantages of EUV lithography are higher costs & complexity (than ArFi lithography) and relative infrastructure immaturity. Source availability and source power at the intermediate focus are not yet at the levels needed for single exposure EUV cost-of-ownership (CoO) comparable to multiple patterning 193i CoO when used for printing at the 7LP node. Resist resolution and sensitivity are close to spec: resist line-width-roughness (LWR) is not. LWR reduction via post processing will almost certainly be required. Mask blank defectivity and yield are continuing to improve: defect repair, defect avoidance, and defect compensation techniques are still needed for finite mask yield and actinic tools are needed for blank inspection, pattern mask inspection, and defect repair verification.

After more than 30 years of development, EUV topics that still need additional work include: source and scanner availability, pellicle transmission, and resist LWR/LCDU reduction. If not addressed, stochastic effects (photon shot noise, resist molecular inhomogeneities, scattering event, etc.) will become the most significant limiter of lithographic scaling.

Presenting Author

Obert Wood is a Principal Member of Technical Staff in the Strategic Lithography Technology Department at GLOBALFOUNDRIES. He was a Member of Technical Staff at Bell Laboratories for 34 years and has extensive experience in extreme-ultraviolet lithography, ultra-high intensity lasers and laser surgery. Obert received his B.S., M.S. and Ph.D. Degrees from the University of California at Berkeley in Electrical Engineering in 1964, 1965 and 1969. He is author or co-author of 271 technical papers and inventor or co-inventor of 27 patents and is a fellow of the Optical Society of America and SPIE, a senior member of IEEE, and a member of the AAAS, the American Physical Society, and the American Vacuum Society.

P2

High Power HVM LPP-EUV Source with Long Collector Mirror Lifetime

(Keynote Presentation)

Hakaru Mizoguchi

Gigaphoton Inc., Hiratsuka Kanagawa,254-8567, JAPAN

We have been developing CO_2-Sn-LPP EUV light source which is the most promising solution as the 13.5nm high power light source for HVM EUVL. Unique and original technologies such as; combination of pulsed CO_2 laser and Sn droplets, dual wavelength laser pulses shooting and mitigation with magnetic field have been developed in Gigaphoton Inc. The theoretical and experimental data have clearly showed the advantage of our proposed strategy. Based on these data we are developing first practical source for HVM; "GL200E". This data means 250W EUV power will be able to realize around 20kW level pulsed CO2 laser. We have reported engineering data from our resent test such around 43W average clean power, CE=2.0%, with 100kHz operation and other data [1)]. We have already finished preparation of higher average power CO2 laser more than 20kW at output power cooperate with Mitsubishi electric cooperation[2)]. We achieved 132W with 100kHz, 50% duty cycle operation during 120 hour[3)]. Recently we have demonstrated short term operation at 264W level open loop operation at proto type #2 system[4)].

We are now operating new high power HVM LPP-EUV source with new CO2 driver laser system made by Mitsubishi Electric. Now we are demonstrating long collector mirror lifetime (< 0.5% down per G・Pulses) protected by our magnetic mitigation system around 100W level (in burst) operation condition.

1) Hakaru Mizoguchi, et. al.: "Sub-hundred Watt operation demonstration of HVM LPP-EUV source", Proc. SPIE 9048, (2014) [9048-12]
2) Yoichi Tanino et.al.:" A Driver CO2 Laser Using Transverse-flow CO2 Laser Amplifiers" (EUV Symposium 2013, Oct.6-10.2013, Toyama)
3) Hakaru Mizoguchi et al.:" Performance of new high-power HVM LPP-EUV source " Proc. SPIE. 9776, Extreme Ultraviolet (EUV) Lithography VII, (March 18, 2016)
4) Hakaru Mizoguchi, et al: "Development of 250W EUV Light Source for HVM Lithography",EUVL Workshop 2016,(Berkley, 13-16, June, 2016)

Presenting Author

Hakaru Mizoguchi is Executive Vice President and CTO Of Gigaphoton Inc. He is a member of The International Society of Optical Engineering, The Laser Society of Japan and The Japan Society of Applied Physics. He received a diplomat degree in plasma diagnostics field from the Kyushu university, Fukuoka, Japan in 1982 and join Komatsu Ltd. He joined CO2 laser development program in Komatsu for 6 years. After that he was guest scientist of Max-Plank Institute Bio-Physikalish-Chemie in Goettingen in Germany 2 years, from 1988 to 1990. Since 1990 he concentrated on KrF, ArF excimer laser and F2 laser research and development for lithography application. He was general manager of research division in Komatsu Ltd. until 1999. He got Dr. degree in high power excimer laser field from Kyushu university in 1994. In 2000 Gigaphoton Inc. was founded. He was one of the founders of Gigaphoton Inc. From 2002 to 2010 he organized EUV research group in EUVA program. Now he is promoting EUV light source product development with his present position.

P3

EUV Lithography for HVM
(Keynote Presentation)

Britt Turkot

Intel Corporation

Recent developments in EUV exposure source technology have provided demonstrated power levels in line with the technology source power roadmap. The exposure source remains the largest contributor to downtime and availability, with the increase in source power requiring consideration of such effects as exposure dose control, out-of-band radiation, etc. There has been significant overall improvement in EUVL infrastructure to better position the technology for HVM insertion; however, improvements in reticle and pellicle infrastructure lag behind those of the scanner and exposure source. Wafer print test data with and without a pellicle demonstrates defect mitigation within the scanner environment, and predictable yield requires continued emphasis on reticles and pellicles including improvements in techniques to detect and mitigate reticle blank and pattern defects.

Presenting Author

Britt Turkot is a senior principal engineer and engineering group leader with Intel's Portland Technology Development Lithography organization where she is the EUV program manager for Intel. She has been with Intel since 1996 after receiving B.S., M.S. and Ph.D. degrees in Materials Science and Engineering from the University of Illinois at Urbana-Champaign.

P4

Tabletop Coherent EUV Sources and Applications: Full Field Sub-Wavelength Imaging at 13.5nm and Materials Metrology

(Keynote Presentation)

Margaret Murnane

JILA, University of Colorado at Boulder and KMLabs Inc.

High harmonic generation (HHG) is the only route for producing coherent laser-like beams spanning the UV to keV region of the spectrum (~1-60nm) in a tabletop-scale setup. HHG provides unique wavelength, polarization and bandwidth selectable, illumination beams for spectroscopy, microscopy and metrology. Over the past two years, these new quantum light sources have made the transition from the laboratory to industry: KMLabs has engineered an integrated EUV source that combines the drive laser, EUV source and beamline: the XUUS (eXtreme Ultraviolet Ultrafast Source). With record flux, pointing, wavefront and intensity stability, as well as industrial-level thermal management and laser beam pointing stabilization, these advances have enabled the first sub-wavelength resolution 13.5nm imaging using any light source,[1] small or large, as well as robust, quantitative, reconstructions of buried layers, periodic objects, and ultrathin film materials properties and electronic structure.[2-4] Real world applications will include nanomicroscopy in support of nanolithography, process control, characterization of self-assembled nanostructures and as well as real-time imaging of functioning nano-enhanced devices.

1. "Sub-wavelength coherent imaging of periodic samples using a 13.5 nm tabletop high harmonic light source," Nature Photonics 11, 259 (2017).
2. "Full characterization of the mechanical properties of 11-50nm ultrathin films: influence of bond coordination on the Poisson's ratio", Nano Letters, Advance Online (2017). DOI: 10.1021/acs.nanolett.6b04635
3. "Imaging Buried Nanostructures using Extreme Ultraviolet Ptychographic Coherent Diffractive Imaging," Nano Letters 16 (9), pp 5444–5450 (2016).
4. "High contrast 3D imaging of surfaces near the wavelength limit using tabletop EUV ptychography", Ultramicroscopy 158, 98–104 (2015).
5. "Beyond Crystallography: Diffractive Imaging with Coherent X-ray Sources", *Science* 348, 530 (2015).

Presenting Author

Margaret Murnane is a Distinguished Professor of Physics and Electrical and Computer Engineering at the University of Colorado. She received her B.S. and M.S. degrees at University College Cork, Ireland and a Ph.D. from UC Berkeley. Her work has led to major practical advances in the technology of ultrashort-pulse lasers and coherent extreme ultraviolet and x-ray sources. Her honors include a MacArthur Fellowship, election to the National Academy of Sciences, and most recently the Ives Medal, which is the highest award of the Optical Society of America. With Henry Kapteyn, she co-founded KMLabs Inc. to commercialize laser and EUV technologies for critical applications in nanoscience and nanotechnology (kmlabs.com). She currently leads a vibrant transdisciplinary research group, and directs a new multi-university NSF Center for Real Time Functional Imaging (STROBE.colorado.edu).

P5

EUV Lithography: Progress in LPP Source Power Scaling and Availability

(Keynote Presentation)

Igor Fomenkov

Cymer LLC, An ASML Company, San Diego, CA 92127, USA

This paper discusses the latest improvements in EUV source performance for semiconductor lithography including power scaling and availability. EUV source power has exceeded the 200W level for the first time, and significant increases in availability have been achieved due to implementation of the latest developments in EUV source subsystems including the tin droplet generator, CO_2 laser and control system.

This paper describes the development of laser-produced-plasma (LPP) extreme-ultraviolet (EUV) sources for advanced lithography applications in high volume manufacturing. We discuss the most recent results from high power testing on our development systems targeted at the 250W configuration, and describe the requirements and technical challenges related to successful implementation of these technologies. Subsystem performance will be shown including Master Oscilator Power Amplifier (MOPA) Pre-pulse operation with high Conversion Efficiency (CE) and dose control with low overhead and high die yield. We describe the most effective optimized modes of operation to control the plasma dynamics at high power and with the necessary collector protection. This presentation reviews the experimental results obtained on NXE 3400B sources with a focus on the topics most critical for a 250W HVM LPP source.

Presenting Author

Igor Fomenkov is an ASML Fellow in Technology Development Group in San Diego, California. After completing a Ph.D. in Physics and Mathematics at Moscow Institute of Physics and Technology (MPTI) in 1986, he joined General Physics Institute as a senior scientist, where he worked in the field of interaction of high intensity laser radiation with matter and diagnostics of laser produced plasma. He joined Cymer in 1992 and worked on the development of high power, high reliability KrF and ArF Excimer lasers for DUV (at 248nm and 193nm) microlithography. Since 1997 he has been conducting research and development of sources for Extreme Ultraviolet Lithography at 13.5nm. He was appointed Cymer Fellow in 2003 and ASML Fellow in 2014. He has authored over 50 technical papers and holds over 100 patents in the areas of DUV and EUV light sources.

P11

kW-class Picosecond Thin-disk Pre-pulse Laser PERLA for Efficient EUV Generation

Akira Endo[1], Martin Smrž[1], Jiří Mužík[1,2], Ondřej Novák[1], Michal Chyla[1], Tomáš Mocek[1]

[1] *HiLASE Centre, Institute of Physics AS CR, Za Radnicí 828, 252 41 Dolní Břežany, Czech Republic*

[2] *Faculty of Nuclear Sciences and Physical Engineering, Czech Technical University in Prague, Břehová 7, 115 19 Praha 1, Czech Republic*

Technology for EUV lithography source is getting matured. >100 W LPP sources have already been in HVM application and 250 W sources are expected to be realized soon. However, further increase of power and cleanness requires a powerful picosecond laser in near infrared and wavelength converted spectral region. Hilase Centre has been working in the thin disc laser technology, and demonstrated a 0.5 kW platform Perla C based on a very compact Yb:YAG regenerative amplifier. The 100-kHz picosecond operation has been achieved with fundamental spatial mode and excellent long-term stability. We present in this talk on a thin-disk based picosecond Yb:YAG solid-state laser technology platform PERLA developed in Czech Republic and the present performance of delivering > 4mJ, <2 ps pulses at 100 kHz repetition rate with potential to be upgraded to 1 kW of average power and 1 MHz pulse repetition rate. The picosecond laser extendibility is critical for >kW LPP source and controlled FEL EUV source for >10kW power region.

Presenting Author

Professor Dr Akira Endo obtained Dr. degree from Tokyo Institute of Technology in 1981 from high power short pulse laser research. He joined in "Extreme Laser Program" of Institute of Solid State Physics, University of Tokyo and performed a research on a multi terawatt excimer laser for XUV source pumping. He continued a similar research in the laser division of Max Planck Institute for Biophysical Chemistry, Göttingen, Germany during 1988-1992 for a conceptual study of Petawatt laser. He was a research leader in METI project "Femtosecond Technology" as a member of Sumitomo Heavy Industries Inc. and responsible for "laser-Compton X-ray sources" during 1996-2002 in Japan. He was then the research leader in the "EUVA" project as a member of Giga Photon Inc. during 2002-2009, and contributed to establish the CO_2 laser pumped Tin droplet LPP scheme for >100W source. He was invited to Jena University as a Zeiss Professor during 2009-2010, and to FZD research center in Dresden. He is now a guest Professor in Waseda University in Tokyo, Japan, and the research leader of the Thin Disc laser program in HiLase Centre in Prague, Czech Republic.

P12

Scalability of CO_2 Amplifiers to Generate Stable > 500W Extreme Ultraviolet (EUV) Beams

Koji Yasui[1],
Naoyuki Nakamura[2], Jun-ichi Nishimae[2],
Masashi Naruse[3], Kazuo Sugihara[3], and Masato Matsubara[3]

[1]Mitsubishi Electric Corporation, Head quarter, Factory Automation Systems Group, Tokyo, Japan
[2]Mitsubishi Electric Corporation, Advanced technology R&D center, Hyogo, Japan
[3]Mitsubishi Electric Corporation, Nagoya works, Nagoya, Japan

Scalability of CO_2 amplifiers to generate > 500W EUV beams that are required in the near future for high-volume-manufacturing of IoT/AI devices are discussed. We consider that with the emerging application fields related to IoT/AI technology, EUV lithography has become essential technology and also road map until the physical atom limit has to be well designed. For the purpose, we have been proposing CO_2 amplifiers with transverse-gas-flow configuration, so that we can enhance laser powers, efficiency, beam stability, and beam shape uniformity. In this talk, several scalable plans are discussed. For instance, the electrical efficiency should be enhanced up to approximately 2 times compared with conventional methods maintaining the good beam shapes required for efficient EUV generations from tin plasma. Digital pre-pulsing is also going to be proposed to increase the EUV generation efficiency.

Presenting Author

Koji Yasui received B.S. and Ph. D. degrees from the University of Tokyo in 1982 and 1989 respectively. He was a visiting scientist at the Stanford University in 1989. He joined Mitsubishi Electric Corporation in 1982, where he has developed high-power CO_2 lasers, high-power solid-state lasers, high-power green lasers, high-power 266nm UV lasers and laser processing machines using those laser sources. He is now working as a senior chief engineer and as a senior chief technologist in charge of laser technology, EDM technology, CNC technology and e-beam technology and related businesses.

P13

Simulating EUV Production – an Overview of the Underpinnings

Howard Scott and Steve Langer

Lawrence Livermore National Laboratory, USA

Numerical simulations are routinely employed as valuable tools in a wide variety of technical endeavors. Using simulations can deepen our understanding of physical systems by providing both a view of details unavailable from experimental diagnostics and the opportunity to improve our understanding and intuition by numerical experimentation. Exercising this opportunity requires the availability of high-fidelity, predictive numerical simulations based on accurate models of the underlying physical phenomena on relevant time and spatial scales.

The microphysics of EUV production from laser-produced plasmas is relatively well understood and models built on this understanding have guided efforts to design more efficient sources. However, most numerical simulations of this process on the macroscopic scale depend on a variety of assumptions and approximations, limiting their ability to predict the performance of any given source. Providing predictive simulations that can reliably guide the development of improved sources will require replacing approximations with more general (but more expensive) computational treatments.

We discuss numerical models of the critical microphysics processes for EUV generation, emphasizing the underlying approximations and corresponding restrictions. We then briefly review current simulation efforts, identifying appropriate usage regimes. Our goals are to understand the applicability of the current simulations and provide guidance on developing computational tools with improved predictive capability.

This work was performed under the auspices of U.S. Department of Energy by Lawrence Livermore National Laboratory under Contract DE-AC52-07NA27344.

Presenting Author

Howard Scott is a staff physicist at Lawrence Livermore National Laboratory where he has been developing simulation codes since 1986. He holds a PhD in astrophysics and has worked in the areas of inertial confinement fusion, magnetic fusion energy, X-ray lasers, nuclear weapons, and even some astrophysics. His particular research interests are radiation transport, non-LTE physics, plasma spectroscopy and large-scale simulations.

P14

Short-pulsed Nd:YAG Laser Interaction with Tin Micro-droplets

O.O. Versolato

Advanced Research Center for Nanolithography (ARCNL), Science Park 110, 1098 XG Amsterdam, The Netherlands

We present our findings on the interaction of short-pulsed Nd:YAG laser light with tin micro-droplets which currently serve as mass limited targets in plasma sources of extreme ultraviolet light. High-quality, high-speed shadowgraphic investigations of the propulsion and deformation of the laser-impacted tin droplet shed light on the underlying plasma physics and as well as the fluid dynamic response which we study in detail as a function of experimental parameters at ARCNL. Spectroscopic investigations, both of the laser-produced plasma as well as in electron beam ion trap facilities at the Max-Planck-Institute für Kernphysik in Heidelberg enable fingerprinting the individual contributions of the various charge states of tin to the spectrum of in-band, and out-of-band radiation.

Presenting Author

Oscar Versolato received his PhD in 2011 from the University of Groningen, The Netherlands, for work on laser spectroscopy on trapped, short-lived radium ions. He did postdoctoral work at the Max-Planck-Institute für Kernphysik in Heidelberg, Germany, on spectroscopy and sympathetic laser cooling of highly charged ions (with PTB Braunschweig, DE), and molecular ions (with Aarhus University, DK).

Since 2015 he is a tenure-track group leader in the EUV Plasma Processes group at the Advanced Research Center for Nanolithography (ARCNL). His present research interests include plasma sources of extreme ultraviolet radiation, physics of highly charged ions, and spectroscopy.

P15

Next Generation Source Power Requirements: What will we need at the 3 nm node and beyond?

Erik R. Hosler

GLOBALFOUNDRIES, 400 Stone Break Road Extension, Malta, NY 12020

As the semiconductor industry approaches EUV high-volume manufacturing insertion, the technology extendibility paths must be assessed. Future process technology nodes and patterning complexity will continue to drive lithography and materials performance to achieve the desired device capability. The impact on machine requirements are clear for tightened EUV lithography performance at 0.33 NA and multipatterning, either the overall throughput is reduced incrementally according to the dose or by integer increments according to the number of exposure passes, respectively. However, high-NA EUV lithography will drive a mixture of increased dose and improved scanner mechanics to maintain throughput due to doubling the number of exposures required per wafer resulting from the anamorphic lens design. Regardless of the next generation patterning strategy, there will be an impact to the scanner throughput capability. Here, the implication to EUV throughput capacity is analyzed within the context of the 7/5/3 nm technology nodes for various lithographic scenarios.

Presenting Author

Erik Hosler is a Member of the Technical Staff in the Strategic Lithography Technology Department at GLOBALFOUNDRIES, and is currently driving EUV industrialization as the lead EUV Technologist. He earned his PhD from the University of California at Berkeley in 2013 in Physical Chemistry, studying ultrafast chemical dynamics with Stephen R. Leone. Since joining GLOBALFOUNDRIES, he has also focused on the exploration and development of disruptive technologies, including the evaluation of free-electron lasers for use in semiconductor manufacturing.

P16

A Compact Linac-Driven EUV Light Source utilizing a Short-Period Microwave-Driven Undulator

Filippos Toufexis*, Cecile Limborg-Deprey, Valery A. Dolgashev, Sami G. Tantawi

SLAC National Accelerator Laboratory
2575 Sand Hill Rd, Menlo Park, California 94025
** Also at the Department of Electrical Engineering, Stanford University*

Conventional Synchrotron Light Sources and Free-Electron Lasers utilize permanent magnet undulators with periods on the order of a few centimeters, requiring electron beam energies of at least 500 MeV to generate 13.5 nm light. We have developed a short-period microwave-driven undulator operating at 91.392 GHz with a period of 1.75 mm. The beam energy required to produce 13.5 nm radiation is only 130 MeV. We are currently modifying the X-Band (11.424 GHz) Test Accelerator at SLAC to operate as an EUV light source. We will replace the existing RF photogun with a thermionic RF injector. The beam is accelerated using two X-Band accelerating structures. The first one is a 1 m-long traveling wave structure, and the second one is a 30 cm-long high-shunt impedance standing wave structure. The 130 MeV beam then interacts with the microwave-driven undulator. The undulator is powered by a 91.392 GHz accelerator structure, which extracts the RF power from the spent electron beam. The length of this system, including diagnostics, is only 6 m. We will present our current design and projected operating parameters for this compact EUV light source.

Presenting Author

Filippos Toufexis received the Diploma of Electrical Engineering from the National Technical University of Athens, Greece in 2011, and the Masters in Electrical Engineering from Stanford University in 2013. He is currently a PhD Candidate in Electrical Engineering at Stanford University, working with Prof. Tantawi on mm-waves and compact light sources. He is further pursuing three PhD Minors in the Departments of Mechanical Engineering, Bioengineering and Aeronautics & Astronautics, at Stanford University. Prior to joining Stanford, Mr. Toufexis worked at Helic, Inc. developing software for integrated inductor synthesis and modeling. This software is used by major semiconductor companies. His research interests include the development of mm-wave/THz sources, compact synchrotron light sources, FELs, and their applications in semiconductor manufacturing, biology and space.

P17

Concept for 1kW EUV Source for Lithography Based on FEL Emission in Compact Storage Ring

Michael Feser

Lyncean Technologies Inc.

Today's EUV lithography scanners are powered by laser produced plasma (LPP) sources. Issues with scaling up the power, reliability and contamination of LPP sources have delayed the introduction of EUV lithography into manufacturing for many years and they continue to be the number one item on the list of EUV challenges to address. Free Electron Lasers (FELs) have been under investigation as an alternative EUV source. Advantages of accelerator based sources are the maturity of accelerator technology, lack of debris/contamination and ability to provide high power. Industry has turned away from this technology because of the requirement to feed up to 10 scanners from one linear FEL to make it economically feasible and the big size and generation of radioactive byproducts. These issues are overcome in the presented concept using a compact storage ring with steady state FEL lasing action. At 1kW output power, comparable cost and footprint to a LPP source this source will be ideally suited for use on a single scanner and promises reliable and contamination free operation. FEL action in the storage ring is sustained by operating the FEL well below the saturation regime and preserving the equilibrium low emittance and energy distribution of the ring.

Presenting Author

Michael Feser is CEO of Lyncean technology. Previously, he was VP in Carl Zeiss X-ray Microscopy and Xradia Inc., Pleasanton, CA. He has experience in X-ray microscopy and computed tomography, X-ray fluorescence imaging / spectrometry, Theory and practice of diffractive, reflective and transmissive x-ray optics, Nanofabrication and characterization and X-ray detectors, complex positioning systems, interferometry. He received a Ph.D. in Physics (2002) from State University of New York at Stony Brook, Stony Brook, NY on the topic of "Scanning x-ray microscope instrumentation and image restoration."

P18

Challenges to Realize the EUV-FEL High Power Light Source - Present Status on the EUV-FEL R&D Activities

Hiroshi Kawata

High Energy Accelerator Research Organization (KEK), Tsukuba, Ibaraki 305-0801, Japan

It is important to develop the high power EUV light source up to 1 kW to realize the 5nm node, which is expected to be in production at 2023-24. To this end, an energy recovery linac (ERL)-based free electron laser (FEL) must be a most promising candidate, so that our group has done some feasibility studies from the view point of accelerator technology. In order to realize the EUV-FEL high power light source, it is also important to recognize the demand of end users and related problems on the FEL light source. Last year, we attended many conferences and workshops to learn these items and also we organized one day workshop "EUV-FEL Workshop" at Tokyo. You can find the presentation materials in a website of http://pfwww.kek.jp/PEARL/EUV-FEL_Workshop/presentaions.html. I would like to present the update on the KEK activities for developing a FEL-based EUV light source and also the summary of the "EUV-FEL Workshop".

Presenting Author

Hiroshi Kawata is the Head of ERL Project Office in KEK, Department of Future Accelerator and Detector Technologies, High Energy Accelerator Research Organization (KEK).

P21

EUV Optics Life-time Research: Past, Present and Future

(Review paper)

Norbert Koster, Edwin te Sligte, Arnold Storm, Herman Bekman, Jacques van der Donck, Diederik Maas, Jochem Janssen, Rogier Verberk

TNO, Stieltjesweg 1, 2628 CK Delft, The Netherlands

In the year 2000 ASML made the decision to start with the development of an EUV scanner as the most likely candidate for next generation lithography. This meant a huge leap in technology development as the tools went from refractive optics to reflective optics and from ambient to vacuum. One enabler of this decision was the invention of the Dynamic Gas lock (DGL) by TNO. This invention solved one of the major showstoppers for EUVL, namely carbon contamination of the optics. The DGL made it possible to separate the "dirty" wafer stage environment from the optics compartment and thus protects the delicate optics from carbon contamination by outgassing of resist.

Since 2000 a large contamination control program is running at TNO to extend optics life time of EUV lithographic tools. In this presentation on optics lifetime research (OLR) we will show results from the past, outline current challenges and present our expectations for future OLR topics for EUV HVM applications. One of the work horses for future EUV optics life time research is the EUV Beam Line (EBL2) at TNO, an open facility that can be used to study photon/plasma/material interaction according to the power roadmap of ASML. Work performed by others will be highlighted during the presentation.

Presenting Author

Norbert Koster is Principal Scientist at TNO and has a bachelor degree in precision engineering. He has worked in vacuum technology and EUV lithography since 1992. Since 1999 he is employed at TNO as lead vacuum engineer and plasma scientist. As such he is involved in projects for EUV Lithography, plasma technology, contamination control, nuclear fusion (ITER) and ion beam lithography. As Principal Scientist, Norbert is also responsible for scientific and strategic programs of TNO and leads several research programs in the department Nano-Instrumentation. These programs are a part of TNO International Centre for Contamination Control of which Norbert is one of the founding fathers. He is a member of the Dutch vacuum society NEVAC, the American Vacuum Society (AVS) and the International society for optics and photonics (SPIE).

P22

The Future of EUV Lithography: Enabling Moore's Law in the Next Decade

Jan van Schoot, Kars Troost, Alberto Pirati, Rob van Ballegoij, Peter Krabbendam, Judon Stoeldraijer, Erik Loopstra, Jos Benschop, Jo Finders, Hans Meiling, Eelco van Setten, Bernhard Kneer*, Bernd Thuering*, Winfried Kaiser*, Tilmann Heil*, Sascha Migura*

ASML Netherlands B.V., De Run 6501, 5504 DR Veldhoven, The Netherlands
**Carl Zeiss SMT GmbH, Rudolf-Eber-Straße 2, 73447 Oberkochen*

While EUV systems equipped with a 0.33 Numerical Aperture lenses are readying to start volume manufacturing, ASML and Zeiss are ramping up their development activities on a EUV exposure tool with Numerical Aperture greater than 0.5.
The purpose of this scanner, targeting an ultimate resolution of 8nm, is to extend Moore's law throughout the next decade.

A novel, anamorphic lens design, has been developed to provide the required Numerical Aperture; this lens will be paired with new, faster stages and more accurate sensors enabling Moore's law economical requirements, as well as the tight focus and overlay control needed for future process nodes. The tighter focus and overlay control budgets, as well as the anamorphic optics, will drive innovations in the imaging and OPC modelling. Furthermore, advances in resist and mask technology will be required to image lithography features with less than 10nm resolution. This paper presents an overview of the target specifications, key technology innovations and imaging simulations showing the capabilities of the next generation EUV systems.

Presenting Author

P23

Latest Developments in EUV Optics

Jack Liddle, Joerg Zimmermann, Jens Timo Neumann, Matthias Roesch, Ralf Gehrke, Bernhard Kneer, *Eelco van Setten, *Jan van Schoot

Carl Zeiss SMT GmbH, Rudolf-Eber-Straße 2, 73447 Oberkochen
**ASML Netherlands B.V., De Run 6501, 5504 DR Veldhoven, The Netherlands*

The NXE:3400 optics created by Zeiss contain many ground-breaking improvements. The reduced Pupil Fill Ratio (PFR), wider sigma range, and decreased aberration of the NXE:3400 enhance the imaging capabilities of the tool in comparison to the NXE:3350. The reduced PFR and wider sigma range of the illuminator extend the ultimate resolution down to 13nm half-pitch. The flexibility of the illuminator supports the realization of freeform SMO pupils on the scanner, provides matching of illumination settings to the NXE:3350, and offers powerful pupil tuning capabilities. The decreased aberration of the projection optics lead directly to contrast, CDU, overlay, and focus improvements. These improvements will be discussed together with application examples.

Beyond the NXE:3400 high-NA EUV optics will support imaging well into the future. We will give an overview of high-NA EUV imaging and development status.

Presenting Author

P24

EUV/SXR Optics and Metrology Development at RITE

Ladislav Pina

Rigaku Innovative Technologies Europe (RITE), Prague, Czech Republic

RITE products are based on 46 years long R&D experience of its experts in the field of replicated X-ray optics. Current development activities and recent results in the field of replicated EUV/SXR optics and imaging detectors are presented. Condensers for EUVL metrology, Water Window microscopy, X-ray cameras for submicron resolution tomography and ultraprecise metrology detector are included. Typical application results are shown.

Presenting Author

P25

Large Collector Mirror Reflectometer for the High Power EUV Light Source Achievement

Takeo Watanabe and Tetsuo Harada

Center for EUVL, Laboratory of Advanced Science and Technology for Industry, University of Hyogo

In extreme-ultraviolet (EUV) lithography, the development of an high power EUV source is the top critical issue. Since the power requirement of the EUV light produced from the laser produced plasma is 250 W at the intermediate focus position. To meet the power requirement high conversion efficiency and a large collector mirror with high stable reflectivity are necessary. For the collector mirror, the EUV output power directly depends on the focusing efficiency of the EUV collector mirror. Thus, the reflectometer for the large collector-mirror reflectance measurement plays an important role to increase EUV source power in the EUV source system. We have developed a reflectometer at BL-10 beamline of the NewSUBARU synchrotron light facility for the measurement of the large collector mirror reflectance. We successfully measured an EUV collector mirror with a diameter of 412 mm with almost 100% *s*-polarization EUV light. The collector mirror performance was measured with a high reproducibility in peak reflectance and CWHM analysis. This reflectometer will contribute for the development of an EUV mirror optics and EUV source system.

Presenting Author

Takeo Watanabe received his Ph.D. from Osaka City University in 1990. He is Full Professor, Director of Center for EUV, and Dean Laboratory of Advanced Science and Technology for Industry, University of Hyogo. He is an expert of the EUV lithographic technology, including optics, exposure tool, mask and resist technologies. He has authored over 200 technical papers, and he is international affair, the organizing and program committee members, of the International Conference of Photopolymer Science and Technology (ICPST). And he is also Vice Chair of organizing committee of the International Conference of Photomask Japan. In addition, he is a member of SDRJ Committee.

P31

Improved Inspection Ability of Coherent Scattering Microscopy by Applying Ptychography

Young Woong Kim[1], Dong Gon Woo[1], Seung Hyuk Shin[2], Hoon Jo[2], Whoi-Yul Kim[2] and Jinho Ahn[1]

[1]Division of Materials Science and Engineering
[2]Department of Electronics and Computer Engineering
Hanyang University, 222 Wangsimni-ro, Seongdong-gu, Seoul 04763, Republic of Korea

Mask inspection is one of the key technologies for the insertion of extreme ultraviolet lithography into semiconductor industry. Coherent Scattering Microscopy (CSM), which is an EUV actinic inspection technology, can reconstruct the image of EUV mask from captured diffraction patterns using phase retrieval algorithm. This can provide several mask information including diffraction intensities, phase information and diffraction efficiency. So the local CD and phase difference can be obtained within the field of view (FOV) of 1.5μm.

Recently, we applied the Ptychopraphic Iterative Engine (PIE) in order to overcome the limit of the small inspection area of CSM. For improvement of inspection ability of CSM, we developed modified PIE such as extended PIE (ePIE) and position correcting PIE (pcPIE) which update the probe function simultaneously and compensate the inevitable position error. Furthermore, we adopted super-resolution PIE (SR-PIE) to improve resolution by extrapolating the recorded diffraction patterns beyond the aperture of the detector. Through the comparison of images obtained by each PIEs, we will demonstrate the applicability of PIE in EUV inspection technology.

Presenting Author

Young Woong Kim is a Master & Doctor course, student under Prof. Jinho Ahn, in the Nano Process & Device Laboratory, Department of Materials Science & Engineering, Hanyang University, 04763, Seoul, KOREA.

P32

RESCAN - A Standalone Tool for EUV Mask Defect Inspection

Patrick Helfenstein*[a], Iacopo Mochi[a],
Rajeev Rajendran[a], Istvan Mohacsi[a], Yoshitake Shusuke[b], Yasin Ekinci[a]

[a]*Paul Scherrer Institute, Villigen PSI, Villigen, CH-5232, Switzerland*
[b]*NuFlare Technology, Inc., 8-1 Shinsugita-cho, Yokohama 235-8522, Japan*

We are developing a reflective EUV mask-scanning lensless imaging tool (RESCAN) for EUV mask inspection. Our system is based on a two-step defect inspection method. First, a low resolution defect map is generated by comparing diffraction patterns from areas with programmed defects to those that are known to be defect-free on our test sample. In a later stage, a die-to-database comparison will be implemented. This technique operates purely in the Fourier domain without reconstructing the aerial image and, given a sufficient signal to noise ratio, defects are found in a fast and reliable way, albeit with a location accuracy limited by the spot size. Subsequently, a fine scan is carried out in the vicinity of these locations. Since our source delivers coherent illumination, we can use an iterative phase-retrieval method to reconstruct the aerial image of the scanned area with – in principle – diffraction-limited resolution.

In order to meet the stringent requirements for high-volume manufacturing in terms of throughput, a potential mask inspection tool requires a continuously moving sample stage and fast frame-rate detector. We will present a novel detector capable of a frame-rate of up to 2 kHz and a dynamic range of > 10^6 for EUV photons and also outline our design for a compact synchrotron source optimized for EUV radiation.

Presenting Author

P33

EUV Mask Economics: Impact of Mask Costs on Patterning Strategy

Bryan S. Kasprowicz[1] and Michael Lercel[2]

[1]Photronics, Inc.
[2]ASML, Inc.

Defect free masks, improved resist sensitivity, increased source power and perhaps larger masks for high NA have been identified as key enablers that need to be improved or resolved before EUV can be implemented as the next patterning technology. Significant industry efforts have identified solutions and many are working towards them. However the increased equipment and mask costs have been seen as an impediment, raising the questions as to whether EUV can be affordable enough relative to multiple patterning that it will foster broad industry adoption.

This paper addresses the most critical costs in producing leading edge masks and the implications on next patterning nodes. Consideration of EUV lithography versus multiple patterning in a manufacturing environment will be addressed.

Presenting Author

P34

NewSUBARU EUVL R&D Activities and EUV Mask Defect Inspection

Takeo Watanabe and Tetsuo Harada

Center for EUVL, Laboratory of Advanced Science and Technology for Industry, University of Hyogo

It is announced that EUV lithography will be used from hp 16 nm electronic device high volume manufacturing around 2018 and 2019 by several device companies at IEDM 2016 in last December.

At the NewSUBARU synchrotron light source of University of Hyogo, 1) large reflectometer for the reflectivity measurement, 2) resist evaluation tool for pattering, outgassing, and chemical reaction analysis tool, and 3) mask inspection tool were developed.

The defect free mask fabrication is one of the big issue of EUV lithography. Since the mask inspection system in high quality is necessary, the EUV coherent scatterometry microscope using HHG laser as a light source had been developed at University of Hyogo. Recently, using this system, the observation of both a defect and EUV mask patterns is succeeded. Then the diffraction image was captured by X-ray CCD camera. The mask defect image was reconstructed on a basis of the coherent diffraction imaging. The details of the recent results are introduced and discuss the benefit of the EUV coherent scatterometry microscope using HHG EUV light.

Presenting Author

P35

Measuring Aberrations with Mask Roughness

Aamod Shanker

Dept. of Electrical Engineering and Computer Sciences, University of California, Berkeley, CA

Speckle produced by a rough mask under EUV light naturally fills the entire pupil of an imaging tool. On recombining with the background field, the speckle intensity at the image plane interferometrically encodes the even part of the imaging tool aberrations in its Fourier spectrum. Additionally, the differential change in the speckle intensity with illumination angle is shown to encode the odd part of the aberration function. Hence the whole aberration can be reconstructed, and subsequently deconvolved from images of a patterned mask for improved resolution. Further, field-of-view dependent aberrations are also retrieved using the local speckle at each position. The method is demonstrated on the SHARP EUV microscope using just a blank mask as the specular object, along with illumination angle diversity. Applicable to any EUV imaging or metrology tool which has speckle from blank areas on the mask, the method allows for in-situ aberration measurement and real-time tool alignment.

Presenting Author

Aamod is a final year graduate student at the University of California, Berkeley, where he is researching phase imaging methods with applications in microscopy and lithography. His undergraduate degree was from the Indian Institute of Technology, Kharagpur, India in 2011.

P36

Impact of Tool Design on Defect Detection Sensitivity for EUV Actinic Blank Inspection

Yow-Gwo Wang,[a,b,*] Andrew R. Neureuther,[a,b] Patrick P. Naulleau[b]

[a]*University of California, Berkeley, Department of Electrical Engineering and Computer Sciences, Berkeley, California, United States, 94720*
[b]*Lawrence Berkeley National Laboratory, Center for X-ray Optics, 1 Cyclotron Road, Berkeley, California, United States, 94720*

In this paper, we discuss the impact of various tool design perspectives on defect detection sensitivity for dark-field based EUV actinic blank inspection. We consider the impact of optical resolution, EUV source type, and photon collection efficiency on defect SNR performance. The results show that as the pixel size approaches the target defect image size, defect SNR increases, and that pixel size also determines the dominant noise source in the inspection system. Moreover, the choice of the EUV source affects the optimal NA and illumination settings. For plasma-discharged sources, more photons provided by larger partial coherent illumination can improve the SNR, while coherent illumination is needed to get a higher defect SNR for synchrotron-based source. We show that simply increasing the photon collection efficiency by using high NA optics or increasing the source power cannot always improve the defect SNR. In a speckle noise dominated situation, larger outer NA includes more noise than defect signal, thus results in a lower SNR. The impact of source power also saturates at a certain level as the system becomes speckle noise-limited. In the end, the system requirements study for future critical defects show that a smaller pixel size and a stronger source power are needed to increase the critical defect SNR.

Presenting Author

Yow-Gwo Wang is a Ph.D. candidate in Electrical Engineering and Computer Sciences at the University of California, Berkeley. He is also a graduate student researcher at the Center for X-ray Optics, Lawrence Berkeley National Laboratory. His current research project is focused on design, fabrication, and testing new concepts for high sensitivity EUV aerial image inspection under the guidance of Prof. Andrew Neureuther and Dr. Patrick Naulleau. He was the recipient of SPIE BACUS Scholarship in 2015.

P37

Rigorous 3D Electromagnetic Simulation of Ultrahigh Efficiency EUV Contact-hole Printing with Chromeless Phase-shift Mask

Stuart Sherwin[a], Thomas V. Pistor, Andrew Neureuther[a], and Patrick Naulleau[b]

[a]*University of California, Berkeley, Department of Electrical Engineering and Computer Sciences, Berkeley, California, United States, 94720*
[b]*Lawrence Berkeley National Laboratory, Center for X-ray Optics, 1 Cyclotron Road, Berkeley, California, United States, 94720*

Achieving high-throughput EUV patterning remains a major challenge due to low source power; phase-shift masks can help solve this challenge for certain patterns by creating brighter images than traditional absorber masks when illuminated with the same source power. Experimentally, a chromeless checker-board phase-shift mask for 25-nm dense contacts has been shown to provide a throughput gain of 8x based on characterization with the SHARP EUV microscope and 7x based on microfield patterning with the Berkeley MET. Building upon these experimental results, in this paper we establish that under idealized Kirchhoff analysis the phase-shift mask should be 2.4x brighter for the minimum-pitch line-space pattern and 5.9x brighter for the minimum-pitch contact array pattern. We then use rigorous 3D Finite-Time Time Domain (FTTD) simulations to quantify 3D mask effects, i.e. deviations from the Kirchhoff model. Finally, we use these simulations to find the offset from the naive Kirchhoff mask design that compensates for these 3D mask effects, finding that this compensation for minimum-pitch lines and spaces in the shadowing orientation entails a 15% deeper etch and a 6% reduction in the mask CD, while the compensation for the minimum-pitch contact array entails a 20% deeper etch.

Presenting Author

P38

Anamorphic Imaging: Emulating Future Nodes of EUV Lithography on the SHARP Microscope

Markus Benk, Weilun Chao, Ryan Miyakawa, Kenneth Goldberg, Patrick Naulleau

Lawrence Berkeley National Laboratory, Center for X-ray Optics, 1 Cyclotron Road, Berkeley, California, United States, 94720

With EUV lithography moving closer to production, the next generation of EUV scanners is already under development. The proposed scanner at 0.55 NA will have an anamorphic projection optic with different magnifications in the x- and y direction. The Semiconductor High numerical aperture Actinic Reticle review Project (SHARP) is a synchrotron-based, EUV microscope, designed to emulate illumination and imaging conditions of current and future generations of EUV lithography scanners. This flexibility is enabled by the use of nanofabricated diffractive imaging lenses that measure less than 100-um in diameter, allowing 100s of lenses to be installed in the tool, and a high brightness source coupled with a lossless Fourier synthesis illuminator. Zone plates with an anamorphic 4x/8x aperture of 0.55 enable the SHARP microscope to emulate anamorphic imaging today. We have run the first user shifts, studying mask effects in anamorphic imaging mode. The paper provides an overview of the SHARP microscope and its key components. We focus on the emulation of anamorphic imaging, presenting a variety of image data. Contrast at high mask-side NA is compared for anamorphic and isomorphic imaging and the transfer of substrate roughness and line edge roughness in anamorphic and conventional imaging modes is discussed.

Funding for SHARP operations and upgrades is provided by Intel. General EUV infrastructure at Berkeley is funded through the EUREKA program. This research used resources of the Advanced Light Source, which is a DOE Office of Science User Facility under contract no. DE-AC02-05CH11231.

Presenting Author

Markus Benk is the project scientist at the SHARP microscope, Center of X-ray Optics, Lawrence Berkeley National Laboratory. He received his diploma in photo engineering from the Cologne University of Applied Sciences in 2006 and his PhD from RWTH Aachen University in 2011. His current research interests include sources, metrology and optics for soft x-rays, and extreme ultraviolet light.

P39

Reduction of Large Killer Defects in EUV Mask Blanks

Adrian Devasahayam, Alan V. Hayes, Boris Druz, Sandeep Kohli, Rustam Yevtukhov,

Veeco Instruments Inc (United States)

Investigation of methods to reduce defects in EUV mask blanks fabricated by Veeco's low defect density ion beam deposition (LDD-IBD) systems is reported. In particular, efforts to minimize "beam overspray," a potentially major cause of "killer" particle defects and elemental contamination, are described. Several factors to reduce "overspray" were evaluated, including chamber pressure, grid ion optic patterns, target shapes, and beam focus. Reduction in beam overspray of up to ~100X was demonstrated. Tool upgrades were developed and tested on the basis of these findings and are available for implementation. One of these upgrades, a new, elliptically shaped grid pattern, was incorporated in a LDD-IBD system at SEMATECH and associated, along with several other improvements, with the production of the first reported defect-free EUV mask blanks at 54 nm inspection sensitivity.

Presenting Author

P40

Variable Separation Method for Three-dimensional EUVL Mask Diffraction Simulation

Xiangzhao Wang*, Heng Zhang, Sikun Li

Laboratory of Information Optics and Opto-electronic Technology, Shanghai Institute of Optics and Fine Mechanics, Chinese Academy of Sciences, Shanghai, China, 201800

Mask diffraction simulations are necessary tools for lithography process optimization such as mask optimization or mask optical proximity correction (OPC). Rigorous electromagnetic method for EUVL mask simulation provides accurate diffraction spectrum but consumes large computing resources (time and memory) especially for Three-dimensional (3D) EUVL mask. Various fast methods have been proposed for efficient mask simulations. In order to achieve better simulation speed and accuracy this paper proposes a fast simulation method based on a decomposition strategy named variable separation. According to variable separation theory, a 3D mask is decomposed into two orthogonal 2D masks. Spectrums of these 2D masks are obtained through rigorous electromagnetic method. The final 3D mask spectrum is the product of these two 2D mask spectrums. Simulation result of contact-hole mask with different contact sizes and mask pitches shows apparent speed enhancement and good simulation accuracy. For 22 nm sized contact hole mask, setting incident chief-ray-angle as typical 6° with 45° linear polarization, and ranging azimuth angle from 0° to 90°, the errors of the simulated critical-dimension of the proposed method are within 0.21 nm compared with the rigorous "Waveguide" method in lithography simulator Dr.LiTHO while the simulation speed is 65 times faster. Under the same simulation condition, the proposed method achieves more than doubled simulation accuracy and simulation speed comparing with the domain decomposition method of Dr.LiTHO. The method has clear physical meaning and suits especially for EUVL contact mask simulation and optimization.

Presenting Author

Xiangzhao Wang received his BE degree in electric engineering from Dalian University of Technology, China, in 1982, and his ME and DrEng degrees in electric engineering from Niigata University, Japan, in 1992 and 1995, respectively. Now he is a professor at the Shanghai Institute of Optics and Fine Mechanics, Chinese Academy of Sciences. His research interests include lithography imaging theory and technology, information optoelectronics.

P41

Reactivity of Metal Oxalate EUV Resists as a Function of the Central Metal

Steven Grzeskowiak,[a] Amrit Narasimhan,[a] Michael Murphy,[a] Lee Napolitano,[b] Daniel A. Freedman,[b] Robert L. Brainard,[a] and Greg Denbeaux[a]

[a] *State University of New York Polytechnic Institute - CNSE, 257 Fuller Rd. Albany, NY 12203*

[b] *State University of New York at New Paltz, 1 Hawk Drive New Paltz, NY 12561*

Traditional EUV photoresists have been composed of organic compounds which are moderately transparent to EUV. Resist stochastics and sensitivity can be improved by increasing the number of photons absorbed. Molecular organometallic resists are a type of metal containing resist aimed at improving EUV absorption. This work focuses on studying the role of the metal center (Metal = Co, Fe, Cr) in an oxalate complex by comparing the number of absorbed photons and the photoelectron reactivity in each compound.

In the study presented here, the EUV absorption coefficients are determined experimentally by measuring the transmission through a resist coated on a silicon nitride membrane using an Energetiq EQ-10M xenon plasma EUV source. Additionally, the photochemistry is evaluated by monitoring outgassing reaction products. This particular resist platform eliminates oxalate ligands when exposed to electrons or EUV photons resulting in a solubility difference between the exposed and unexposed regions. In the process, carbon dioxide is produced and is monitored using mass spectrometry, where quantitative values are obtained using a calibration technique.

For the metal oxalate complexes studied, the absorption of EUV changed minimally due to the low concentrations of metal atoms. However, EUV and electron reactivity greatly changed between the three compounds likely due to the reducibility of the metal center. A correlation is shown between E_{size} and the reducibility of each photoresist.

Presenting Author

Gregory Denbeaux is Associate Professor in SUNY POLYTECHNIC Institute in Albany, NY.

P42

Towards Real-Time Analysis of Morphologies using Scattering

Alex Hexemer

Lawrence Berkeley National Laboratory, Berkeley, California, United States, 94720

The advent of high brightness sources, fast detectors and the increasing need of time-resolved experiments in small angle scattering has created an unprecedented data deluge and the needs for combining X-ray science with computer science. Over the last few years we have worked closely with our computational research and supercomputer division to enable the use of supercomputers at scattering beamlines. The dream of such a *superfacility* would be immediate feedback for scientist during experiments. To step closer to that goal we have developed a plug-in based toolkit that connects algorithms and allows execution on fast clusters and supercomputers. We have developed a variety of high performance plug-ins as well as developments of analysis tools in collaboration with scientist from around the country. The main focus is the determination of small feature morphologies from X-rays. We will highlight two recent developments for gratings. First the inclusion of CD-SAXS in our framework for fast and user friendly execution and second the development of a high performance gracing incidence code to simulate and fit grating shapes. We will show some recent results and comparison.

Presenting Author

P43

Novel EUV resist development for sub-7 nm node

Yoshi Hishiro

JSR Micro INC, 1280 N. Mathilda Ave, Sunnyvale, CA 94089, USA

Extreme ultraviolet (EUV) lithography has been recognized as a promising candidate for the manufacturing of semiconductor devices as LS and CH pattern for 7nm node and beyond. EUV lithography is not to be ready for high volume manufacturing (HVM) stage. For the HVM of semiconductor devices, significant improvement of sensitivity and line edge roughness (LWR) and Local CD Uniformity (LCDU) is required for EUV resist. It is well-known that the key challenge for EUV resist is the simultaneous achievement of ultrahigh resolution (R), low line edge roughness (L), and high sensitivity (S). Especially high sensitivity and good roughness are very important for EUV HVM. We have been trying to improve sensitivity and LWR/LCDU in many aspects and directions. Material study found that both sensitivity and LWR/LCDU are simultaneously improved by controlling acid diffusion length and efficiency of acid generation using novel resin and PAG. Stack Integration is one of the good solutions to improve sensitivity and LWR/ LCDU. We have been challenging to develop new multi-layer stack materials to improve sensitivity and LWR/LCDU. Our new multi-layer materials are designed for best performance in EUV lithography. Process study found that sensitivity was substantially improved while maintaining LWR by applying novel chemical amplified resist (CAR) and process. In this paper, we will report the recent progress of sensitivity and LWR/LCDU improvement of JSR novel EUV resists and processes.

Presenting Author

P44

Extreme ultraviolet Induced Chemical Reactions in Photoresists and Model Systems

S. Castellanos[a], Y. Zhang[a], J. Haitjema[a], L. Wu[a], O. Luigier[a], D. Kazazis[b], M. Vockenhuber[b], T. R. Fallica[b], Y. Ekinci[b], A.M. Brouwer[a].

[a] *Advaced Research Center for Nanolithography, Science Park 110, 1098XG Amsterdam, The Netherlands*
[b] *Paul Scherrer Institute, 5232 Villigen PSI, Switzerland*

Hybrid inorganic-organic materials are considered the next step in materials for extreme ultraviolet (EUV) photolithography. At ARCNL we investigate how variables defined by the molecular structure affect the reactivity of this kind of materials towards EUV light. For that purpose, we have prepared a series of compounds with rationally controlled variation of structure and composition to test their efficiency in EUV-induced pattern formation. This set of materials include Sn-based organometallic compounds[1] and Zr- and Hf-based metal-oxoclusters.[2]

Our investigations revealed that the absorptivity of the model compounds follows the expected trends based on the atomic cross-sections of the elements they contain. Thus, Sn-based model photoresists exhibit the highest values, close to commercial EUV photoresists.[3] Nevertheless, the sensitivity suggested by EUV interference lithography[4,5] does not correlate with the absorptivity trends. The study of the photoproducts indicates different mechanisms of solubility switching for Sn-based metal-organic compounds[6] and Zr- and Hf-based oxoclusters as a result of their distinct composition and chemical bonding. This investigation can have important implications in the design of a new generation of EUV photoresists.

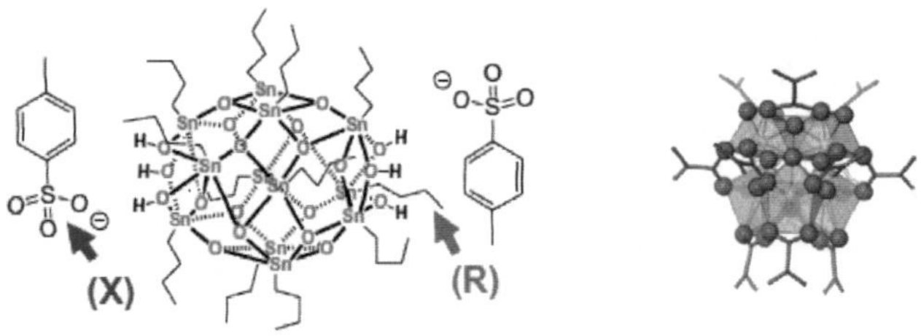

Figure 1. Schemes of the Sn-based (left)[5] and Zr-based (right)[2] model photoresists tested with EUV interference lithography.

[1] Banse, F., Ribot, F., Toladeno, P., Maquet, J., Sanchez, C., *Inorg. Chem.* **1995**, 34, 9.
[2] G. Kickelbick, U. Schubert, Chem. Berich. 1997, 130, 473; S. Gross, G. Kickelbick, M. Puchberger, U. Schubert, *Monatshef. Chem.* **2003**, 134, 1053
[3] R. Fallica, J. Haitjema, L. Wu, S. Castellanos, A. M. Brouwer, Y. Ekinci, Proc. SPIE Vol. 10143, 101430A;
[4] J. Haitjema, Y. Zhang, M. Vockenhuber, D. Kazazis, Y. Ekinci, A. M. Brouwer, Proc. SPIE Vol *10143*, 1014325
[5] Cardineau, B.; Del Re, R.; Marnell, M.; Al-Mashat, H.; Vockenhuber, M.; Ekinci, Y.; Sarma, C.; Freedman, D. A.; Brainard, R. L. *Microelectron. Eng.* **2014**, 127, 44.
[6] Y. Zhang, J. Haitjema, X. Liu, F. Johansson, A. Lindblad, S. Castellanos, N. Ottosson, A. M. Brouwer, Proc. SPIE Vol 10146, 10146-5

Presenting Author

Sonia Castellanos Ortega received her PhD in Chemistry, awarded with an Extraordinary Prize, from the University of Barcelona in 2010 for her work in the design and preparation of organic radicals with applications in electronic devices. During her postdoctoral stage in HU Berlin she conceived novel photoswitchable organic molecules to modulate the rates of light-to-electron conversion in the frame of an Alexander von Humboldt fellowship. Right after, she worked in the development of photoresponsive metal-organic frameworks as a postdoc in TU Delft. Since February 2016 she is the group leader of the EUV Photoresists in the Advanced Research Center for Nanolithography in Amsterdam.

P47

EUVL Developments at Imec

Greg McIntyre

IMEC

This talk will give an overview of some of the activities at imec focused on enabling the industry's insertion of EUV, with particular focus on photoresists, masks, pellicles, and advanced patterning techniques. IMEC's activities range in scope between understanding fundamentals to bringing ideas from the lab to fab, to demonstrating concepts relevant to high-volume manufacturing. Imec's activities with respect to photoresist development will be discussed, where imec has a broad program engaged in exploring novel materials platforms, understanding fundamentals of image formation in CARs and Non-CAR materials, screening materials, understanding stochastics and developing post-processing techniques (i.e. roughness smoothing), and studying contamination & manufacturability concerns. This talk will also touch on recent advances in photomask defectivity and imaging, where imec has been developing a CNT-based pellicle solution which has demonstrated excellent properties for optical transmission, mechanical strength, and chemical and thermal durability, and is believed to be scalable to future manufacturing needs. Additionally, advancements with alternate mask absorbers will be discussed, demonstrating both the need and a viable path for thin Ni and Co based mask films. Lastly, an overview of imec's thoughts on EUV insertion will be provided, with results from various N5 and N3 use-cases for EUV.

Presenting Author

P48

Fundamental Aspects of Low Energy Electron Driven Chemistry

Dan Slaughter

Chemical Sciences Division, LBNL

In chemically amplified EUV resist materials chemical modifications, such as acid generation, will be driven primarily by the emitted electrons. Absorption of an EUV photon can ionize valence and inner shell electrons in a resist material and, in the latter case, Auger electrons can be emitted as excited molecules decay. Primary photoelectrons and Auger electrons typically generate secondary electrons by inelastic scattering with molecules surrounding the EUV photoabsorption site. Each absorption and scattering event can produce reactive species by dissociation, ionization and electron attachment. The design of a good EUV photoresist requires a fundamental understanding of these processes.

Gas-phase experiments provide valuable insight into the fundamental processes that occur in condensed phase systems. Mass-spectrometry and photoelectron spectroscopy (PES) techniques applied to gas-phase systems can be used to gain understanding of primary and secondary processes occurring in resist materials. Anion fragment mass spectrometry experiments allow us to measure the dissociation channels and their relative yields following attachment of low energy electrons to molecules relevant to chemically amplified photoresists. I present the results of recent experiments to investigate these processes.

Presenting Author

From 2014-present Dan is a Staff Scientist at Chemical Sciences Division, Lawrence Berkeley National Laboratory. In 2007 he received his PhD from Flinders University, Adelaide, Australia. His PhD Thesis was titled "Superelastic Electron Scattering from Caesium."

P50

Metal Oxide Photoresists: Breaking Paradigms in EUV Lithography

Jason Stowers

Inpria

To meet the challenging patterning requirements for EUV lithography, Inpria has developed an entirely new class of photoresists based on metal oxide materials. One of the significant differences between conventional resists and MOx based resists is the inherently high etch contrast of the latter relative to other layers in the stack. Having what amounts to a hard mask at the top of the lithography stack results in a variety of additional degrees of freedom for integration. This can encompass the straightforward reduction of layers in the patterning stack or enable entirely new integration flows that leverage the etch properties of a MOx resist. In essence, MOx resists are EUV photo-patternable hardmasks. In this presentation, we discuss process integration opportunities unlocked by Inpria's MOx resists, which provide enhanced image fidelity post-etch with simpler processes.

The performance of MOx resists stems from a photopatterning mechanism entirely distinct from that of conventional chemically amplified resist materials. Inpria has developed a molecular scale Monte Carlo model for our MOx systems. This model provides the appropriate descriptive language and a framework for understanding how these resists function as well as how different processing conditions affect the resist performance. Here, we review our model and how it guides our design process.

Presenting Author

Jason Stowers is a Principal Engineer at Inpria. He received his Ph.D. from Oregon State University in inorganic chemistry. During his graduate work, he developed novel inorganic photoresist materials which formed part of the core technology on which Inpria was founded. He was a member of the initial startup team and has been actively involved in EUV lithography for 12 years.

P51

Estimation of Lithographically-relevant Secondary Electron Blur

Roberto Fallica and Yasin Ekinci

Paul Scherrer Institute, 5232 Villigen PSI, Switzerland

The spatial distribution of secondary electrons generated by EUV photons ins a resist material is of paramount interest but still far from understood. Recent works estimated that a cascade of 10 electrons is generated, on average, per absorbed photon at EUV (with incident energy of 91.9 eV). It is generally agreed that these low-energy (i.e.< 10 eV) electrons can travel through the resist at distance of several nanometers away from the initial absorption location. As a result, secondary electron blur is not just an elusive and poorly understood phenomenon, but also an important factor for resist sensitivity and a major limit to the ultimate resolution in EUV lithography. In this work, we present a quantitative measurement of the effect of the secondary electron blur which becomes lithographically relevant when patterning very thin films. Our approach is the experimental observation of their spreading. The experiment exploits the discontinuity of absorption and thereby the secondary electron distribution which occurs at the resist/substrate interface when a different wavelength is used to expose the material. We aim for elucidating the secondary electron blur, which expresses itself as a shift in clearing dose at the proximity of resist-substrate interface due to changing energy and absorption.

Presenting Author

Roberto Fallica graduated in Electronics Engineering (M.Sc.) from Politecnico di Milano in 2007. In 2012 he completed the PhD School in "Nanotechnology and Nanostructures" at the Department of Materials Science of the University of Milano-Bicocca with a thesis on the electrical characterization of chalcogenide nanowires. He previosly worked at the National Research Council of Italy and he is now a postdoctoral researcher at the Paul Scherrer Institute (Switzerland), where he conducts research on Extreme Ultraviolet lithography patterning and fundamentals.

P52

EUV Lithography Research and Development Activities at University of Hyogo

Takeo Watanabe and Tetsuo Harada

Center for EUVL, Laboratory of Advanced Science and Technology for Industry, University of Hyogo

EUV resist which satisfy high resolution, high sensitivity, low LER, and low outgassing, simultaneously is one of the technical issue of EUV lithography for high volume manufacturing,

At NewSUBARU synchrotron light source of University of Hyogo, 1) the resist absorption coefficient measurement in high precision using photodiode, 2) EUV resist chemical reaction analysis using total electron yield method, 3) EUV interference lithography for the evaluation of 1X nm patterning, 4) resist outgassing evaluation tool using in-situ ellipsometry, and 5) 1st principle calculation method applied for the chemical structure analysis of the polymer resist material were prepared.

Using these tools, total EUV resist characteristics such as resolution, sensitivity, outgassing, and chemical reaction can be evaluated in one facility. In the poster session, the recent results will be introduced.

Presenting Author

P61

Coherent diffraction imaging with partially coherent discharge plasma based EUV sources

Jan Bußmann[1,2], Michal Odstrcil[1,3], Raoul Bresenitz[1], Yusuke Teramoto[4], Marco Perske[5], Torsten Feigl[5], William S. Brocklesby[3], Larissa Juschkin[1,2*]

[1] Chair for Experimental Physics of EUV, JARA-FIT, RWTH Aachen University, Steinbachstrasse 15, 52074 Aachen, Germany
[2] Peter Grünberg Institute 9, JARA-FIT, Forschungszentrum Jülich GmbH, 52425 Jülich, Germany
[3] Optoelectronics Research Center, University of Southampton, SO17 1BJ, United Kingdom
[4] BLV Licht- und Vakuumtechnik GmbH, Steinbachstraße 15, Aachen, Germany
[5] OptiXfab. GmbH, Hans-Knoell-Str. 6, 07745 Jena, Germany

Coherent diffraction imaging (CDI) is a powerful method with a broad range of applications in nanoscience, material science and biology. It offers a possibility of either avoiding the imaging optics or including their limited quality into the image reconstruction process. Additionally, it allows for recovering both phase and amplitude of the exit-wave field behind the sample. This results in much higher contrast for phase objects that would have otherwise low contrast in standard bright field microscopy. We report on lens-less imaging experiments including also scanning probe (ptychographic) CDI with compact plasma radiation sources developed for EUV lithography applications. Two kinds of discharge sources have been used in experiments, a hollow cathode triggered pinch plasma source operated with oxygen or xenon and a laser assisted discharge EUV source with a liquid tin target. The CDI reconstructions of different samples were achieved by applying constraint relaxation to the CDI algorithm. The developed linear relaxation method can handle the low spatial coherence and broadband nature of the source radiation as well as the residual background due to visible light emitted by the plasma. The resolution down to 100 nm is demonstrated and is limited presently by the sample structure contrast and exposure time. Our results show that compact plasma-based EUV light sources of only partial coherence can be effectively used for lens-less imaging applications. We show first results and propose an experiment for CDI using a reflective setup and a compact xenon-discharge based EUV source. Our special focus is put on demonstration of actinic diagnostics of multilayer mirrors modified by programmed, buried defects. Coherent diffraction imaging can recover the phase and amplitude change induced by the buried defects. This information is not accessible by other methods or at other inspection wavelengths and facilitates further development and improvement of the multilayer fabrication process.

Presenting Author

P62

Achromatic Talbot lithography with partially coherent EUV radiation

Sascha Brose[1], Jenny Tempeler[1], Hyun-su Kim[2,3], Serhiy Danylyuk[1], Peter Loosen[1], Larissa Juschkin[2,3]

[1] Chair for the Technology of Optical Systems, JARA-FIT, RWTH Aachen University, Germany

[2] Chair for the Experimental Physics of EUV, JARA-FIT, RWTH Aachen University, Germany

[3] Peter Grünberg Institute 9, JARA-FIT, Forschungszentrum Jülich GmbH, Germany

In this contribution, we present the EUV laboratory exposure tool. It is a versatile patterning tool suited for many applications in academia and industrial research, reaching from pre-patterning of substrates to resist and pellicle characterization. The setup consists of a discharge produced plasma source with a direct beam path to a phase-shifting transmission mask, the photoresist coated wafer and the positioning system. High throughput is enabled by the utilization of the achromatic Talbot effect that is suited for broadband emission, since all radiation contributes to the interference pattern. The method also allows for a two times demagnification of the mask features, leading to more relaxed mask fabrication requirements. For process window identification, systematic exposure series were performed varying the mask-wafer distance and the exposure dose. The depth of field is found to be 20 μm in close proximity to the transmission mask. Optimization of the exposure parameters resulted in 35 nm half-pitch wafer features with low defectivity level. The process window can be extended by spatial filtering techniques, leading to sub-30 nm wafer half-pitches.

Presenting Author

P63

Spectroscopic EUV reflectometry for characterization of thin films and layered structures

Maksym Tryus[1], Serhiy Danylyuk[2], Daniel Wilson[3], Stefan Herbert[2], Lukas Bahrenberg[2], Angelo Giglia[4], Piergiorgio Nicolosi[5], and Larissa Juschkin[1,3]

[1] Chair for the Experimental Physics of EUV, JARA-FIT, RWTH Aachen University, Germany
[2] Chair for the Technology of Optical Systems, JARA-FIT, RWTH Aachen University, Germany
[3] Peter Grünberg Institut 9, JARA-FIT, Forschungszentrum Jülich GmbH, Germany
[4] CNR - Istituto Officina Materiali, Trieste, Italy
[5] Dipartimento di Ingegneria dell'Informazione, Universita' degli Studi di Padova, Italy

Modern nanotechnology is continuously raising demands on quality and purity of thin films and interlayer interfaces. As thicknesses of employed layers decrease to single nanometers, traditional characterization tools struggle to satisfy simultaneously throughput, precision and non-destructibility requirements. Spectroscopic reflectometry with extreme ultraviolet radiation (EUV, 5-40 nm wavelengths) offers a possibility of non-destructive study of surfaces. To this end, EUV spectroscopic reflectometry has been employed as a non-destructive metrology tool, which also allows controlling in-depth structure of the produced materials. We report on a series of reflectivity measurements on the samples of interest, e.g. different high-k thin films, that has been performed using our tabletop Polychromatic Angle-resolving Non-destructive Tool for High-speed Extreme-ultraviolet Reflectometry (PANTHER). Reflectivity spectra of the probed materials feature characteristic absorption edges with their fine structure. Near-edge x ray absorption fine structure (NEXAFS) analysis of some materials can therefore be realized in the EUV range to gain additional information about chemical composition. Collection of spectral "fingerprints" and analysis of near-edge reflectivity of samples have been done additionally at the ELETTRA synchrotron facility, Trieste. The experimental and analytical results along with the outlook on the development of the method will be presented and discussed. In addition to that, a suitability of the tool to the industrially relevant applications such as analysis of surface contamination, will be illustrated by results of experiments with test samples exposed to real EUV source operation environment. The technique shows high chemical sensitivity and correlates with photoemission electron microscopy results.

Presenting Author

P64

EUV scattering metrology: Benchmarking of discharge plasma source based table-top scatterometry versus PTB synchrotron based EUV radiometry

Oleksiy Maryasov[1,2], Christian Laubis[2], Mewael Sertsu[1,3], Frank Scholze[2], Larissa Juschkin[1,4*]

[1] Chair for the Experimental Physics of EUV, JARA-FIT, RWTH Aachen University, Steinbachstr. 15, 52074 Aachen, Germany

[2] Physikalisch-Technische Bundesanstalt (PTB), Abbestraße 2-12, 10587 Berlin, Germany

[3] Dipartimento di Ingegneria dell'Informazione, Universita' degli Studi di Padova, Italy

[4] Peter Grünberg Institute 9, JARA-FIT, Forschungszentrum Jülich GmbH, 52425 Jülich, Germany

Optical scatterometry is a powerful technique for surface roughness metrology and profile characterization of nano-structured layered surfaces. Besides being a fast, non-contact and non-destructive method, it provides spectrally resolved data on the roughness power spectral density (PSD). To demonstrate the feasibility of EUV scatterometry in a user laboratory, we accomplished EUV light scattering experiments on rough, periodic and quasi-periodic nanostructured surfaces at grazing incidence angles (2° - 10°). A high brightness EUV plasma source operated at 1 kHz was used in our compact laboratory tabletop scatterometer setup. Different periodic structures with pitch sizes down to 100 nm were investigated. Up to 15 diffraction orders were observed at 5° grazing reflection from a test gold coated holographic reflecting grating. It shows that resulting scattering signal emerging after grazing reflection of EUV from rough surfaces at 13.5 nm can be recorded in reasonably short times (from 5 s to 10 min) with a high-brightness gas discharge source. We have also applied grazing incidence diffuse scattering measurements in the EUV spectral range at 13.5 nm wavelength for characterization of surface roughness of multilayer coated surfaces and performed benchmarking experiments at the PTB EUV reflectometer. The agreement between the synchrotron radiation based measurements at PTB and laboratory scatterometry is within the expected margins, mainly determined by the sample inhomogeneity and different size of measuring beam footprint for both instruments. The results demonstrate strong sensitivity to a period and roughness of investigated surfaces.

Presenting Author